THE STARSOLUNA GUIDE TO DATING A VIRGO

StarSoLuna Press

Copyright © 2025 StarSoLuna Press

All rights reserved

The information in this book is for entertainment purposes, and not intended to replace therapy, relationship counseling, or the power of self-awareness paired with humor. May you find your love story in the Stars!

No part of this book may be reproduced, or stored in a retrieval system, or transmitted in any form or by any means, electronic, mechanical, photocopying, recording, or otherwise, without express written permission of the publisher.

ISBN-13: 979-8-218-70289-2

Cover design by: Marlo Zivic
Library of Congress Control Number:
Printed in the United States of America

To Marlo,
The most oh-so-Virgo daughter anyone could ever ask for.
May all your suitors heed this guide,
May you always follow your heart,
and may you wear gloves while washing dishes.
With love,
Your Virgo Mumma

CONTENTS

Title Page
Copyright
Dedication
Decoding the Virgo Mindset   4
The Virgo Love Language…   6
Caressing Virgo's Constructive Criticism   8
Swept Off Their Feet, For the Wrong Reasons…   11
VERY Virgo Dates & Gifts   13
Compatibility Guide: 17
Astro-Dating   19
Books In This Series   22

CONTENTS

1. Decoding the Virgo Mindset
2. The Virgo Love Language
3. Caressing Constructive Criticism
4. Swept Off Their Feet
5. Oh-So Virgo Dates & Gifts
6. Virgo's Veritable Match
7. Astro-Dating
8. Conclusion

VIRGO SUN SIGN OVERVIEW

- Dates: August 23 – September 22
- Element: Earth
- Modality: Mutable
- Ruling Planet: Mercury
- Symbol: The Virgin
- Polarity: Yin (Feminine)
- Associated Glyph: A stylized "M" curled inward, suggesting purity and introspection

---

- Birthstone: Peridot
- Flower: Morning Glory or Buttercup
- Signature Colors: Sage green, beige, warm neutrals
- Lucky Day: Wednesday
- Famous Virgos: Beyoncé, Zendaya, Keanu Reeves, Florence Welch, Blake Lively

Virgos are known for their quiet strength, impeccable taste, and subtle charm. Ruled by Mercury, their minds are sharp, their standards high, and their hearts loyal. If you're dating one..., consider this your initiation guide.

DECODING THE VIRGO MINDSET

Virgos have sharp minds and big hearts. They're observant, caring, and a tiny bit perfectionist (okay, maybe more than a tiny bit...). This chapter will unlock the mysteries of their marvelous Virgoan ways.

Your Virgo partner genuinely believes there's a "correct" way to load dishes into a dishwasher. (Spoiler alert: *it's most definitely not your way*.) They approach life with a keen eye for detail, high standards, and a deep commitment to making everything work well - whether it's your wardrobe, or the pillows on the living room couch.

Key to maximizing what will be an incredibly supportive, sensual and romantic relationship is not to take their critiques personally; it's just their unique brand of love.

Relatable Moment: "The Weekend Trip Spreadsheet" Imagine a weekend getaway planned by your Virgo partner —complete with a detailed itinerary, color-coded packing lists, and weather predictions. You might laugh, sigh, want to roll your eyes... but you'll never leave your phone charger, or your favorite razor, behind again!

Virgo FAQ:

- Do Virgos really notice everything? Absolutely—even your mismatched socks.
- Is there a wrong way to fold towels? 100%. Ask your Virgo partner.

Quiz: Are You Fluent in "Virgo"?

- Do they rearrange the dishwasher after you've loaded it?
- Do they send you calendar invites for casual hangouts?
- Do they carry an emergency stain remover?

THE VIRGO LOVE LANGUAGE...

(aka: What really revs a Virgo?)

Hint: Acts of Service, Lists, and Detail-Oriented Romance)

Virgos show their love through meticulous attention and practical actions - thoughtful gestures lead to ultimate romance. To impress a Virgo, actions will speak louder than words. Take something off their plate *and* do it well? Now you have the key to the deeply loving and passionate heart of a Virgo...

Checklist: "Virgo-Wooing Acts of Service"

- Clean their car (and don't skip the cupholders)
- Prepare a thoughtful homemade meal ("You cook, they clean" usually guarantees a lovely evening;)
- Offer to run errands or grocery shop (with their exact list)

Relatable Moments:

- Remember the last time they reorganized your sock drawer without asking? Sure, it

felt invasive, but admit it—it's easier to find matching socks now.
- Is there a wrong way to fold towels? 100%. Ask your Virgo partner

CARESSING VIRGO'S CONSTRUCTIVE CRITICISM

Virgo's critiques are their quirky love language. This chapter teaches you how to handle their perfectionist pointers with charm and wit. Virgo's feedback comes from a place of love (and observational superpowers). Remember, it's not personal—it's practical. Respond with humor and charm and turn these moments into opportunities for closeness.

Virgos take worrying seriously—planning brings them comfort. Clear, reliable plans calm their mind and heart. Understanding their anxiety as a need for order and mental peace rather than criticism changes everything.

Astro-Dating Reality Check: Virgos critique because they genuinely care. On the flip side, admitting when they arc wrong can be a challenge for this sign. Our best advice in love and war?

Practice: Staying grounded, calm, creating a safe space for your Virgo partner to re-assess and analyze their stance. In a healthy relationship marked by self-reflection, they should come to you with a warm, gracious apology - one that feels oh-so-very Virgo!

Quick Tips:

- Humor diffuses tension and can encourage a stressed-out Virgo to relax. (Please don't lose hope - often registering as shy and reserved, Virgo's CAN and DO have fun! And when they get a taste of it, all they really want is more;).
- Patience, and gratitude go a long way (because, appreciating their copious amount of positive productivity is a bonding thing).
- Feeling critiqued from all sides? A gentle "Ah, Virgo-approved (fill in the blank)?" can lighten the mood instantly and works wonders for just about any topic...

Relatable Moment: The infamous grocery list showdown...When your Virgo partner scrutinized your "freestyle" approach to shopping. Instead of defensiveness, turn their precise grocery (and bagging order!) preferences into playful bonding moments. Best to simply get ahead of it with a witty retort. "Ah, Virgo-approved veggies only?" can lighten the mood instantly.

SWEPT OFF THEIR FEET, FOR THE WRONG REASONS...

(aka: "Navigating Virgo Anxiety")

Astro-Dating Reality Check: Virgo anxiety isn't personal, nor is it a ding on you —it's about their relentless pursuit of perfection which on most days, lifts the lives of everyone around them. Offer clear plans, gentle reassurance, and practical solutions. A calm, supportive, and organized partner helps a Virgo feel secure and loved.

Virgo Anxiety Kit:

- **Clearly communicated plans**
- **Gentle, direct reassurance, a comforting hug (don't rush it!)**
- **Thoughtful snacks to quell a hangry Virgo** (think healthy nuts, fresh smoothies, teas, or organic treats)

Practice: "Planning Perfectly"...Create a reassuring action plan template to ease your Virgo partner's anxiety in stressful situations.

This might look like: Providing "When/Where/What to Wear" details for date preparation. With this information, Virgo will be super excited to spend time with you, and of course, they'll have all the information they need to bring their gorgeous A- Game to a great, romantic date - whether it's to a bowling, a biergarten or a ballet.

Relatable Moment: "The Picnic Panic"....When your perfectly Virgo-planned picnic was unexpectedly rained out. Instead of spiraling into anxiety, you produced an umbrella, snacks from your bag, and a smile, instantly making you their superhero.

VERY VIRGO DATES & GIFTS

Dating a Virgo means mastering the art of thoughtful gifting and meticulously planned dates. They can be smitten and wooed with good manners, considered gestures and intentional expressions of love.

Astro-Dating Reality Check: Virgos may like it luxe, but it's geniunely not about lavishness! Rather, Virgos have a keen eye for the intersection of beauty and function - even their personal style generally reflects a pared down, high-quality aesthetic; well-tailored lines, natural fabrics, and classically chic over trendy any day.

Even above fancy gifts, Virgos appreciate a pulled together appearance. This means paying attention to looking *your* best while in their company will make you an appreciated and unforgettable partner in love and life!

Very-Virgo Dates:

- Farmer's market stroll (Have patience, they will likely want to photo-document every, perfect pile of peaches!)

- Art & design museum visit or gallery hopping (Yes, allow them time to browse the gift shop, even if it means another cup of coffee from the cafe for you!)

- Serene afternoon tea date (Don't forget to wear

an irresistible scent and soft cashmere sweater if you're hoping for an evening extension;)

Very Virgo Gift Ideas:

- Elegant planners or journals

- Luxurious, natural skincare products (Just getting to know one another? A posh, travel sized hand-sanitizer fits the Virgo bill for cleanliness on the go;).

- Gourmet, organic granola or premium tea sets

- When it comes to flowers: you can't go wrong with a single flower and monochromatic vibe - this is a bouquet the Virgoan aesthetic will happily integrate into their beautifully curated environment.

- The Virgo Birthstone is Peridot - a green semi-precious stone that is said to help this sign not be so clingy;). Keep jewelry simple and elegant, and if you're not ready for that step - show you know your Virgo stuff with a beautiful green glass decorative object or vase - anything an earth-conscious Virgo can add to their carefully edited home decor.

Very Virgo Dates & Gifts Cont'd.

- Ready to show big love? Your Virgo will return from a Yoga Retreat relaxed and as Zen as Sound Bowl - ready to both give, and receive, love.

Relatable Moment: That time you took your Virgo to an art gallery. Whew...you might not have been prepared for their charmingly detailed analysis of every piece, but you can't deny the eye! Your thoughtful gift of a beautifully designed planner or a sleek journal afterwards showed not only your attentiveness, but made their heart flutter, too.

COMPATIBILITY GUIDE:

(Virgo's Veritable Match)

Quick-glance compatibility ratings for Virgo:

- **Perfect Matches:** Capricorn, Taurus, Pisces
- **Fun but Challenging**: Scorpio, Cancer, Leo, Gemini, Libra
- **Brace Yourself:** Aries, Sagittarius, Aquarius

♥**These Sun Signs +Virgo = A Celestial Path to Love**

- **Taurus:** Practical, reliable, and equally meticulous. Together, they'll build routines they both adore.
- **Capricorn:** Driven, ambitious, and organized, they complement Virgo's desire for structured excellence.
- **Pisces:** Sensitive and dreamy, Pisces is Virgo's relaxing antidote to "all work and no play".

- **Not one of the above?** Follow this guide, and your Virgo love is sure to thrive!

Compatibility Guide Cont'd:

Relatable Moment: Ever watched your Virgo debate with an Aquarius or Sagittarius? It's a "Zodiac Circus" - a comedic battle of organization versus chaos and kinetic movement. There may be lots of playful banter, but there's a lot of star dust between their galaxies!

ASTRO-DATING

(Keeping it Real & Fun)

Astro Reality Check: Astrology should always be playful, fun and enlightening—not stressful. Here's how to gently keep your Virgo grounded when stars overwhelm reality:

- Balance astrology insights with practical relationship wisdom (Virgos are quite rational, after all.)

- Remind your Virgo partner that love isn't about perfection—it's about growth, patience, and support.

- Ensure your needs are met, too! Afterall, hardworking, do-gooder Virgo loves to know when they are "getting it right", so be sure to let them know how to speak *your* Astro Love Language!

Keeping Astro-Dating Fun & Real Cont'd:

Relatable Moments:

- Ever reassured your Virgo after reading a stressful horoscope? Humorously, and with as much wit as you can muster, remind her the celestial stars offer insights—not ironclad predictions.

- When Mercury retrograde gets blamed for Wi-Fi drops, gently tease with, "Maybe Mercury just hates our internet provider?" When in doubt, keep things humorous and grounded.

Conclusion:

Loving a (Perfectly Imperfect) Virgo

You've survived the StarSoLuna Guide and are now equipped to appreciate, understand, and deeply connect with your Virgo partner. Dating a Virgo means appreciating detailed itineraries, carefully planned dates, and lovingly organized chaos. In return, you receive a fiercely loyal, deeply caring partner with whom to create a fulfilling romantic relationship embued with beauty and a touch of earthiness. Your paths have crossed to support the Virgo journey (be they Sun, Moon or Rising); showing them that love isn't about honed perfection, rather it means embracing quirks and imperfections while allowing for mutual growth.

Congratulations on officially becoming StarSoLuna-certified Asto-Dating material! You're ready to love your Virgo fully and imperfectly. Here's to neatly folded socks, perfectly synced calendars, and a love story written in the stars.

BOOKS IN THIS SERIES

The StarSoLuna Survival Guide to Astro-Dating

A fun, lighthearted and giftable series of Astrology-inspired books filled with dating and relationship advice for the 12 Zodiac Sun Signs.

The Starsoluna Survival Guide To Dating A Virgo

Want to nurture a successful romantic relationship with a Virgo? The StarSoluna Survival Guide has you covered! Filled with communicating tips, "oh-so-Virgo" date ideas and heart-felt celestial wisdom, this book offers a fun approach to loving everything this "perfectly imperfect" Astrological sign has to offer.

www.ingramcontent.com/pod-product-compliance
Lightning Source LLC
Chambersburg PA
CBHW051351040426
42453CB00007B/512